Preso

David M. Robert

Cadmus Publishing
www.cadmuspublishing.com

Copyright © 2022 David M. Robert

Cover art by Tad M. Bomboli

Published by Cadmus Publishing
www.cadmuspublishing.com
Port Angeles, WA

ISBN: 978-1-63751-224-1

All rights reserved. Copyright under Berne Copyright Convention, Universal Copyright Convention, and Pan-American Copyright Convention. No part of this book may be reproduced, stored in a retrieval system, or transmitted in any form, or by any means, electronic, mechanical, photocopying, recording or otherwise, without prior permission of the author.

Preso is the Spanish word which means "prisoner." I am about to explain my reason for choosing this as my title. An inmate or convict are given those titles due to their being housed for a crime they committed. I am a prisoner because I'm being held against my will for a crime I didn't commit.

My name is David M. Robert. I plan to take you on a journey. This journey began many years ago. I start this with a poem by an unknown author:

It's so easy for you to criticize me, just by the things you hear.
But what exactly do you know about me to make you say the things you say?
To understand me is to enter my mind, and live my life day today.
You would understand my reason and logic For the decisions that affect each role
You would play the cards you are dealt Even when the words uttered are cold.
You would re live my past experiences as They constantly play and rewind.
You would be faced with my choices and Suffer the consequences that linger behind.
So, when I hear people ridicule me, I never hold a grudge—
Because if they could see the world through My eyes,
they wouldn't be so quick to Judge!!

Preso

I started with this to pervade your minds as you read the following pages.

Before we proceed allow me to begin by stating the fact that I am autodidact. I have book knowledge and street knowledge. This can be a scary combination in the wrong hands. I'm also a firm believer of never being too old to learn things. Many people as they age allow their pride to stagnate their learning. I give all praise and honor to God who has circumcised my heart. God instilled the knowledge within my mind to become a certified paralegal with distinction along with advanced certification specializing in criminal law. I'm also a certified tutor. I just recently completed a social mentoring program. I have more, but this isn't about what I've accomplished while imprisoned. The main purpose of this book is to expose the injustice done to me. The charge I have been accused and charged with I didn't commit. I would be lying if I said I was a model citizen. I have done many things that are contrary to the law.

There are many that can attest to this and some are even eyewitnesses to the stupid things that I've allowed the devil to manipulate my mind into doing. Some may consider a few things I've done as legendary, but I consider them as foolish. I'm ashamed instead of being proud. God has brought me through so much. I can never thank Him enough. God tried to get my attention throughout many different situations I was involved in. I did as most do today, shrugged it off as being lucky. I'm grateful that God has shown me better. Even though I have lost three generations of motherhood while in here their prayers have been answered. In the book of Genesis, Joseph was falsely imprisoned Genesis 50:20 says "But as for you, Ye thought evil against me; but God meant it unto good, to bring to pass, as it is this day, to save much people alive." This is one of the first passages God spoke to my heart. The D.A's office thought evil against me, but God had a greater purpose.

 Although this book has just begun, God is getting someone's attention because they know the man I once was. While being held in the county jail, a guy was extradited from California. I moved him into the cell with me because the others were taking everything, he had due to his charge. When I say everything, I mean e-v-e-r-y-t-h-i-n-g! He was about a minute from being sodomized when I intervened. While in the room with me, we read the Bible throughout the day. At the time, I didn't realize his purpose because he would always try to argue about the Bible. One day during an exchange of words he used the "B" word. I instantly hit him in the face while telling him I was going to kill him. He was placed in an isolation area. During which time he tried to slit his wrists. I kept telling him not to do that. Thank God he finally stopped.

Maybe a day or two later after he's back in population, he comes to me asking me to pray for him. He then proceeds to tell me about things from my past which were impossible for him to know. Next, he tells me that he was a demonic worshipper sent to deter me from following Christ. He says a path had been made for me in the prison system to continue the devil's work as I did on the streets. I dictated quite a few people's thoughts and actions. He goes on to say that he knows that I didn't commit the crime I'm accused of. He spoke of another guy that would come to get him for not completing his mission. The guy came just as he said. The guy tried to disrupt our Bible study a few times but was not successful.

Psalms 55:22 says, "Cast thy burden upon the Lord and He shall sustain thee. He shall never suffer the righteous to be moved. "God's promises are to everyone that loves and obeys Him."

A few years into this time while attending a church service when the service after the invitation for prayer was called a man placed his hands on me and said, "The crime you are in here for you didn't commit." He then tells me God would deliver me. He never said how long. This minister wasn't from Mississippi either. This was the second conformation from God not many years into my imprisonment. Before I proceed to give God Glory, I want to address my main purpose of writing this book. I want to enlighten you to the injustice of wrongful imprisonment which has occurred to me. I will start with me being detained for 345 days before going to trial. There's a statute of limitations in which a person being held should be tried. The time limit is 270 days. I have verification of this. While being housed in Winston-County, which wasn't the county the crime occurred, I called my brother.

As soon as the operator connected us, my brother said, "Where do you want us to come pick you up?"

I replied, "I'm still locked up!" He then proceeds to tell me that the news broadcast stating the charges had been dropped due to the key witness admitted to lying. The D.A.'s office knew they were supposed to release me. This is another violation. The proper procedure was to release me and arrest me when a sufficient indictment was obtained. This charge of homicide should be eradicated and immediate release from imprisonment ordered. Next, one of the state's witnesses testified on record her that she saw the shooter. After being asked if she saw him now, her response was no. I was sitting right there. Her son also admitted to seeing the shooter which wasn't me. That's why the state didn't call him to testify. The deputy in charge of lineup investigation wasn't called because it would reveal I was never identified as the shooter.

The woman who testified spoke of being threatened by the actual shooter about her testimony. It couldn't have been me because they had me in custody already. She wasn't found until the last day of trial due to her fearing for her life. I have a copy of both statements. In every murder case a certain number of pictures are to be presented at my trial. During trial the state produced a fabricated and possibly forged statement which says I admitted to killing the guy. I know for a fact I didn't sign that statement. I even mentioned this to my lawyer. Why would I admit to killing someone and go to trial knowing I would receive a life sentence? Only a mentally disturbed man would do that. The state didn't give me a copy of the indictment until the first day of trial, another violation.

I noticed that it was flawed and showed it to the lawyer. He asks me who had seen it. I presumed that he would keep it and use if things didn't go well. I couldn't make a copy. He took it to the D.A., and they altered it. Yes, they did. After careful examination you can see it has been tampered with. My lawyer admits to showing it to the D.A., another violation on record but claims he took it to him for another reason. Yes, I can prove this too. I know this all seems unbelievable, but it isn't. The day after I was found guilty the lawyer came to me and said, "You really didn't do it, did you?" I replied. "I've been trying to tell you that the entire time." Leading questions are prohibited. I have evidence of this on record because the witness was lying, so the prosecutor had to lead her to get her story right.

The D.A.'s office saw her committing perjury, so they started coaxing her as to what to say. A few years into this time I wrote the lawyer for assistance. During which time I asked for help because he knew I didn't do it. I said, "If anyone could help me it would be him." This due to him allowing me to be railroaded. Through a family member he stated for $20,000 he could get me out. I contacted my brother who paid $5000 as down payment. Unbeknownst to me, my brother didn't give him any more cash. Just as I was about to be barred, I received a letter from the lawyer who informs me of the deadline and says I must finish it myself because he hadn't received ant more cash. By the grace of God, I finished everything and sent it in before the deadline. God is good. In 2006, I was granted an evidentiary hearing. I have paperwork from the Supreme court stating my case meets "Strickland vs. Washington" which is the case that must be met to claim "ineffective assistance of counsel."

Cases meeting this standard are usually overturned. When I went back for the hearing, the police chief of the town knew me. He said, "I heard they have to give you a new trial. Why don't you help yourself out and tell me about a murder that recently happened?"

I replied, "I don't know anything." He says, "Don't give me that I know you know what's going on out there." As you can see that new trial never occurred, I'm still imprisoned. I don't claim to be innocent of any crimes, just this one. I recently learned there is no record of this hearing in my files. Uniform Civil Rules Practices of Circuit and County Court Practices rule 1.12 states, "no record or any part of a file of court papers shall be taken from the clerk's custody without a written order from the judge to the clerk. The clerk shall keep a register of all files checked out by permission of the court and the same shall be redelivered to the clerk on the day provided for in the order from the judge or if none is provided before the opening of the next term."

Now according to this nothing should be missing. I wrote the clerk asking for a copy of my files in its entirety. That's how I found it out. Yes, there's a reason its not there. A new trial would expose the injustice done unto me and there wouldn't be a trial. There's absolutely no evidence proving I did this. Between 2010 and 2014 I was transferred to Greene County. While there I met a guy from where the incident occurred. He asked me to call his family to make sure his Christmas package had been ordered. During the phone conversation, the woman started asking me questions. One was, how much time do you have left? I told her I was in here for a crime I didn't commit. I then talking about it and she says, "You' re right, you didn't do it. I was kin to him." I had made the call through another female which heard the entire conversation.

The next day I go back to the guy known as "Peanut" I wanted to know if she would sign an affidavit to what she said. Her husband snatched the phone from her in the process of me asking. He told me she wasn't going to get in her family business. He then hangs up in my face. The D.A.'s office had been trying to connect me to many other crimes. I was even told if I didn't leave town, they would get me one way or another. I moved to Texas for a few years. While in town I came upon a roadblock. The officer ran my license which came back"10-10". But my passenger had his gun on the seat which was registered. The policeman left and came back to the car with his gun drawn telling me to put my hands up. He then says, "You've got to be drunk!" He arrests me for D.U.I. without even a breath test or anything. I get to the station and attempt to bind out. I'm told I can't be due to a hold from Texas. After forth-eight hours, I'm allowed to bond out. I don't think it was twenty-four hours later, I hear the police are looking for me.

I exclaim, "That can't be true, I just got out!" I call and tell them my location. Minutes later gun wielding officers are outside as if I was a fugitive, armed and dangerous. Rewind to when I first got out, I was trying to do right. The devil knew I wasn't strong. He threw everything at me including the sink and toilet. Most of the day I had went without doing my favorite past time, drinking, and smoking. By night fall I had fallen back into sin. (Ecc 5:4-5) I also learned that most of the agencies that are supposed to help, don't help. It wouldn't take much because I can assist through most of the paperwork. God as kept me throughout the entire 23 years. I am a living testimony of the power of God. I haven't been in a physical altercation the duration of my time behind these walls. I have done time in three of the roughest prisons in the state.

I've done time in Parchman, Wilkinson County and Greene County. God allowed me to be in the worst buildings and zones. Also, I've seen just about everything that goes on.

There's an analogy that I have used before that I would like to share with you. I feel its befitting. Picture about eight to ten guys in here conducting a secret meeting weekly. It's a secret because it's about escaping the prison. The speaker has contemplated an escape plan. Each of those in attendance are listening, "Will this really work?" At one particular meeting, a guy that actually escaped from this prison is in attendance. I'm certain that meeting everyone will be attentive and focused on his every word. Why? Because they know he's actually done it. Often when ministers come to prison to bring the word, the devil speaks to most saying he don't know he's never been through what I have. The devil uses this as a tool.

Many guys behind these walls may not want to admit it, but this thought has crossed every one of our minds. There isn't much that I haven't experienced the time that I was free. Ezekiel 36:31 speaks to me especially. I had a heart of stone. I was selfish and heartless only thinking about myself. I must apologize to the many women I manipulated before I gave my life to Christ. Also, to the many lives I affected negatively. The enemy instills a very rapacious spirit inside most of us. We choose whether or not to it permeate our spirit and souls. My main focus or writing this was to shed light on the injustice done to me. I couldn't leave out the source of my light though. God is my reason for being able to give this testimony. God is going to use this to get me some help that I may become a blessing to others. He deserves all glory and honor.

There is much more that I can testify of God's goodness. If anyone would like to know more or read more, feel free to contact me. I will write more if anyone is interested. I will end this with a quote from Albert Einstein, "There are two ways to live your life., one is as though nothing is a miracle. The other is as though everything is a miracle."

May God bless the reader and writer of this book.

DAVID M. ROBERT

THE END

www.ingramcontent.com/pod-product-compliance
Lightning Source LLC
Chambersburg PA
CBHW071918070526
44583CB00016B/2048